Elemental

Palewell Press

Elemental

Poems - Michael Tanner

Elemental, Poems – Michael Tanner

First edition 2020 from Palewell Press, www.palewellpress.co.uk

Printed and bound in the UK

ISBN 978-1-911587-36-1

We acknowledge with thanks John Blight (of The Camelford Gallery) whose Pen and Ink drawing of Roughtor, Bodmin Moor, we have used on the Front Cover. The drawing was photographed by Alan Burgis of Camelford.

A CIP catalogue record for this title is available from the British Library.

Acknowledgements

Some of these poems were first published by: an baner kernewek; Country Life Magazine; Macmillan Education Ltd.; Poetry Life; Palewell Press; United Press Ltd.; Arrival Press; Wey Poets; Salmon Poetry; Barnet Borough; Elmbridge Borough. The author gives his sincere apologies to any publishers who have inadvertently been omitted.

Stop press news: Michael Tanner is included in the Long List of competitors' results for the 2020 Erbacce International Poetry Competition. There were 9000 submissions from around the world.

Dedication

These poems are dedicated to Mavis, who led me back to Granite Country, and to Gilbert Luther, who died in France, 1916.

Contents

THE PROCESS 3

    Kite Dawn 4

    Cornish Lane 5

    Elemental 6

    Reconciliation 8

    Voice of Gaia 10

    To Hedera helix with respect 12

ENCOUNTERS 13

    Moment of Fox 14

    The Visit 15

    Encounter on a rainy evening 16

    Rooks above Lanteglos Church 18

    Tricks of the Light 19

    Roughtor 20

    Pipistrellus pipistrellus 22

    Gratis 23

WARNINGS 25

    Visitation from Anax imperator 26

    Ambulance 27

    Landfill Site 28

    Chalk Ridge 30

    The Threat 32

    Turdus philomelos 33

    Streetwise 34

    Magpies 36

Gulls on a Football Pitch 37

ELEGAIC 39

Ode to a Cohabitant 40

Relic of War - 1 41

Relic of War – 2 – Resurrection 42

Due Process 44

Lacrimae Rerum (the tears of things) 46

Last Journey of Thomas Bewick's Swan 48

The Quiet Side 50

Master Class 51

When The Wild Geese Fly that Way 52

Frugality of a Bird 53

ARMORICA (Cornwall across the Sea) 55

Misty summer Sunday morning 56

Glow Worms 57

Canticle of the Tidal Mud 58

Refugees 60

Touching the primordial 62

ELSEWHERE 63

Signs and Selfies 64

Silver Birches outside Moscow 65

Hot day on the Embankment 66

Unsolved 67

Incident at Noon 68

Urban Ecology 70

Ecumenical Moment 72

Rural Canvas 74

THE TESTING SHORES 77

    A Slanting Land 78

    Wool on the Wire 79

    Exhibition in Port 80

    Raven's Gratitude 82

    Fulmar 83

    Estuary 84

Michael Tanner – Biography 86

    Palewell Press 86

Foreword

Sunlit spring day on the edge of a North Cornish moor: a man is leaning over the parapet of a stone bridge, mesmerized by the chortling, clinking stream, peering down a shaft of light at all its glints and gleams, movement: green hair of weed combed by the current, flickering silver of minnows, flecks of pyrites gold in the broken granite smoothed for centuries by gravity and waterborne grains of sand. That is my title in a nutshell.

I have been most fortunate to live in this country with its amazingly diverse geology, probably the most varied in the world for such a small area. Even more fortunate to live in an area of Chalk while still so close to an area of Granite. These two geologies and their intimate relationship with the people, flora and fauna of the two regions through their influence on topography, landscape, buildings and local culture constantly remind me of that relationship. Perhaps it is epitomised by the coasts of each area and by their high places, which lift the spirit and humble at the same time. I have a debt also to that English instinct which has enabled so many unassuming footpaths to traverse the South east – the veins of these areas.

The Palewell Press clearly announces its principles and I am flattered by their invitation to come in, but I have rarely sat down to write a poem to promote a definable cause: epic poets do that, and Blake seems to have done so. If my poems do promote the cause of environmentalists and practicing ecologists I am delighted but should confess that that is coincidental in my case. In that respect I think I have much good company. I have written many prose articles on environmental issues, unavoidably marshalling facts and figures provided by the good people who have this particular talent – that is hard, hard work. I cannot pretend that writing poems is not hard, but what a consuming joy.

Words, like children stream into the head's room, get in the way, wear one out but, in the beautiful silence afterwards, one is grateful they came in. Not all my poetry directly relates to the natural scene; green is not the only colour that the human eye creates. I am most grateful to Palewell for their company along the road.

Michael Tanner

THE PROCESS

Kite Dawn

What does she see
this windless March morning,
banking in widening circles
over the curving down,
each feather of her being
trimmed to the element of air:

debris of flint and chalk
fashioned under a sea
now shattered, scattered
by frost and plough;
the crouching hare;
petals of hedgerow violet
stirred by the bumble bee;
the raised face of a man
who studies how,
whatever her need,
page upon page she scans
from east to west -
a book wide as horizons?

Cornish Lane

Lower than fields' level,
winding beyond childhood
along a plane revealed
down centuries to roots and feet.

With mists and stillness
nurturing unsophisticated flowers,
inducing wren to sing,
intruder to listen.

Forgetting destinations,
time of day,
learning to love the inconvenience
of contours, the intention of strata,
you feel out the forms of hills.

Gull and buzzard read
the sentences you inscribe
on a landscape in hazel and thorn
scarped by a sea wind
which snatches their cries.

Here, only runnel's whisper,
wren's song.

Elemental

Leant on this parapet
above a moorland stream,
watching and hearing
ceaseless orchestration
of water caressing rock –
two entities,
such seeming opposites
played on by light and air
pleasing to eye and ear,
focusing thought
as music can.

Gold, copper, tin
seam these hard hills,
beneath their coat of peat,
catching the falling sea
returning it to salt.

Peering down shafts of sun
into the stream below,
I see how water bends
back to me silver and gold –
pyrites, darting minnows,
bubbles on moss
glinting, unassayed flecks.

A planet cools,
vapour to magma,
rock to clay,
to dust,
circling again to life,
leaf, flesh and bone –
the watcher's own.

Water on rock,
rock under water,
opposites
in timeless consummation –
theme of the music
of a moorland stream,
this luminous, listening
timeless afternoon.

Reconciliation

Picture postcards,
family snaps:
freeze-dried memories –
passports to a never-never land
of faces and places,
changing too slow
for shutter speeds
though schooled to smile.

Look at this landscape now,
this perfect sunlit hour –
How did it fend
through seasons without your care,
without your being there?
And all those pictures of children
no longer angel-faced,
no longer with us here?

Today, as yesteryear
these hills and vales,
hedgerows, fields, horizons -
the estuary gleaming
as tide reclaims land?

Towers of antique churches
where villages still hide,
proclaim they have kept faith,
are still the same,
have not left home.

What do you want:
that landscapes, children,
all things move with you
within your kindly
or unkindly ken?

But listen -
the lark that sings,
says clearly every spring,
as do the blossoms down the lane,
even the rock behind the fern –
'There's nothing of any kind
that stays the same.'

The oak, the butterfly,
the ant, the stars, the sea
all have their given pace
but for a jot
of what our kind call 'time',
share being with being
each in its given guise.

So I philosophise,
and now stand
silenced,
wondering at swans
come with the creeping tide
to flower again
upon this salt
but verdant pastureland.

Voice of Gaia

You may plant me
cut me down
make your patterns of fields
roads villages towns
your horizons of concrete and steel
drain seas
move mountains
send toys into what you call Space
like a child who wants to find out.

But I am the Process,
from way beyond your 'biosphere'
to depth of magma
depth of your sun.

Call me what you will
I am the Process
and we all,
fungus, ant, whale, protozoa,
butterfly and even you
the so called articulate one
are part of that whole
promoting or fouling it up
as you think you desire.

10

So young in your thoughts
as in your time
in this place you call world
and such a strange sense
of what you call 'beautiful'
what you call 'wrong'
what you call 'right'.

But putting your labels on things
will not create what you call 'Life'
not make what you call 'Death' –
those palisades you love to build.

To Hedera helix with respect

Insinuating plant
so crooked in your course
from clutching soil
to beckoning sky
so quietly ambitious
the uninvited guest
who pays no fees
enjoys a hostile press.

How imperceptibly
you veil identities
names of the dead
contours of castle and cot
the wealth-announcing plaque
our mortal fripperies!

Yet perfumed flowers
your miniscule stars
herald a winter crop.
Hearth fires sleep in your stems;
your leaves are sustenance
even for lambs.

They say you bring old trees,
old buildings to their knees
but worthy you are to be
Patron of Mountaineers
Archangel of Wrens.

ENCOUNTERS

Moment of Fox

When sometimes you pause
in your easy gait
between here and there
and give the house
a long, considering stare,
I, behind glass,
watch with a quickening heart
trying to catch
before you part,
the essence of your being,
knowing I never shall.

You are elusive
as cloud shadow
passing over wheat,
yet wise enough
to recognise
how like yours
a human heart may beat.

The Visit

In a pale sherry sun
of the twelfth month
I am blessed with goldfinches.

Here in my garden
amid the stalks
of long dead lavenders
heavy with seed,
without preamble
intently, silently they feed
as though time
were about to be called.
The sun touches their symmetry
of crimson and gold.

Suddenly, somewhere,
as one,
they are gone,
leaving a tinkling music
and perfumed defecation
on the stone.

Encounter on a rainy evening

Roe-deer, three, I think, but
colour of dead bracken,
tall, dead reeds
where woodland
turns to marsh.
At dusk, one is not sure of anything.

They see me first –
Two-legged Man,
bulked out in waterproofs,
clumsy through puddles and mud
until He stands,
still as a post,
a post that's watching them!
Caution and curiosity
govern the four of us.

And then I mimic calling of a thrush:
"Again Again Again"
through trees, through rain
sounding not quite bird,
not quite Man.

For seconds more
they linger at the scene
but are not reassured
and vanish into dusk
with virtuoso leaps
except for one
who covers their retreat.

No dogs, no shouts, no gun --
I think they'll not go far,
before they pause
to check they're rid of me,
stooping their slender necks
once more to nibble shoots
while night and rain
establish their domain.

How long they will
recall the event
I cannot say.
One of the two-legged kind
sharing with them
the time of day
and that odd calling
with its strange refrain,

might leave some imprint
on a wild brain.

Rooks above Lanteglos Church

Heath-Robinson affairs these rooks,
launched at the year on strung-together wings
by some creator with no time for looks,
forced to make-do with odd, abandoned things.

Not pretty birds for summer-petalled thoughts,
they work the elements with storm-tried sails,
shouting the hazards to their leaguered ports
before the fury of approaching gales.

Tricks of the Light

Here, on this almost-island
shipwrecked land
where sky and sea
yearn for each other,
someone has laid
white innocence
of sheep and gull
on cloth of grass.

Light hones needles of gorse,
squeezes gold for its flowers,
alizarin for wet clay,
black for cormorant's wing,
slate's blue-grey
onto her morning palette
then slips between
paper and brush.

Roughtor

The sign read two miles and a half –
I found you infinitely further,
emerging from the bronze-age mists
of frontier moors
whose sentinels were momentary
furze bushes and ghosts of sheep.

Even on clear days
when windy sky defines
your bastion strength
and buzzards arc above
in anchored sweeps,
the clambering tourist
has a sense of being watched
and his loud car left at your foot
seems now a toy
too frail to make a get-away.

The high jets weave your skies
rim to horizon rim.
Scientists probe your flanks
with subtler surgery
than their crude ancestors.
But you endure to rhythms
too vastly slow to move
the needles on their clever dials.

Night is your element when,
through the dark of space,
cold stars commune
with your cold stones
and men become mere dreams.

Pipistrellus pipistrellus

Frail flitterer,
Pipistrelle,
spreading your sails
at dusk
beneath emergent stars,
on fingers
fine as veins
in a dead leaf.

Gratis

Sodden, sullen, leaden -
a New Year's English afternoon:
footpaths of trampled mud
strata of rotting leaves
puddles with shores –
sour dough of an afternoon
weighs down the close of New Year's Day.

Then from the snatching hedge
as rain comes with the dusk
and home seems far
a benediction for the parting day
begins with sweetest sotto-voce note,
a lingering bar or two
released unbidden
from a hidden
Hedge sparrow's
fragile, pulsing throat.

WARNINGS

Visitation from Anax imperator

On this bright afternoon
of our carbon-burdened
Post-industrial Age,
you quarter my backyard
from fence to tidy fence
on rigid, rustling wings
veined like the skeletons
of last year's leaves.

What buried stratum
unlocked its sorcerer's book,
released the imprint
of your ghost, which now
feeding on daylight and air
assumes this dreadful imago?

Why have you chosen
this uncertain hour,
seeking what prize
held in the marvel
of your terrible eyes?

Ambulance

Christmas, New Year
shoved into bins with bottles,
glitter dust, needles of fir,
cracker jokes,
Recollections of resolutions.

Like a Christmas tree
half-collapsed
before a child:
main road leans out of town,
hung on the left
with red rear lights ascending,
and on the right
with white front lights descending.

Then shocking, sudden,
out of the dark,
at very top of the tree,
a fairy blue as Arctic ice,
pulsing, cackling,
riveting every sense:
"So you thought
you would leave me out.
We'll see about that!"
And down she sweeps,
between the red and white,
lodging a splinter of ice
in every beating heart.

Landfill Site

Beyond the conurbations
near nowhere in particular
they're seeking to conceal
what happens.
Like hearses at a crematorium
the cargoed lorries
queue at the gate.

Unceasingly
throughout the day
machines regurgitate the land.
At night
palely, a flame bears witness
to what has passed.

They say the work will complete
in a week or two;
engines will judder to silence;
the high gates will be chained.
Ant and worm may then return
to their thankless toil.
A new map is ordained.

But today a west wind
sweeps from the weald
swirling dust
presaging rain
buoying a host
of gulls and crows,
demented chorus
in black and white.

And here you must stand
on their stage,
accept their wailing choreography
Antagonist, Protagonist elect.

Chalk Ridge

Each Spring, touched by pale sun,
this plough-land hatches flints:
They crouch amidst thin corn
preened by the rain,
yet nothing is heavier, more hard,
so tempts the palm
to balance its weight,
savour contour and edge –
How well it fits the hand!

And Shakespeare's Bloody Sun
playing its part above the hill,
reddens a myriad flints with its distemperature
transmuting drops of water on the green
to drops of blood about these dragon's teeth.

I stoop and grasp.
(How readily the arm converts to weapon
swung by Old Gravity!)
look for a target -
giant or too pert shepherd boy
will do.
(Did Cain, surrounded by such possibilities,
wait till a trusting dove
delivered him the trick?)

The rain, foretold, comes down –
I quit the field.
In only four months' time
this crop will cover all
beneath its Cloth of Gold.

Under the hedge I shiver
knowing a thousand years
will not dissolve these flints
nor skies of supplication, ever.

Each Spring, naked they lie –
as readily to hand,
as indestructible,
as thinly buried,
unconfessed desires.

The Threat

What are you waiting for, Woods,
so still in your congregations
in your temples to sun and moon?
Perhaps you are praying.

Now in this month of May
with its thrushes and gentle swaying
why do I feel you are still,
as when your roots slept
beneath leaves frosted and sere?
Do you feel the unstillness near?

White bones of badger and fox
the once rustling shrew,
hermit and tramp,
soldiers,
children long lost
feed your flowers of spring
while you drink in the sun and the sky?

It can't be my wandering through
asking What? asking Why?
while you wait
with a stillness transcending
surf of wheels,
doom impending.

Turdus philomelos

Who, in our slumbering suburb,
understands a thrush?
It throws its sweet abuse
to dawn-grey streets;
casts eggs, sea-stained
for perfect nests from mud;
startles a lawn-soothed eye
with stigma'd breast;
dies before cats and boys –
Picasso's steed
screaming at Guernica.

Streetwise

Saturday morning,
coffee shop in town
favoured by the emphatic young:
Words, like squash balls,
fly forwards, backwards,
sideways, upways,
down into coffee cups,
careless or cunningly aimed,
glancing off facets of meaning,
thudding home or away
with or without invitation.

Spent caffeine-fuelled breath
mists up the windowpane.

On its side of the glass
Street waits;
with tunnel vision, waits;
with fortitude of stone
on rammed foundations;
with Law's, with maps'
authority, waits.

Fat chance has flesh and blood
craving a little tenderness
from cobble stones.

Strait-jacketed in paving,
mortar and flint,
between clenched teeth

Street mutters
'Move along there,
KeeeeP moving!'

with a street's patience
waits for the early hours
of utter emptiness –
no stumbling vagabond,
no club-foot, pecking pigeon,
no creaking sign,
not a soul heeding
the silly struck hour,

dreams of somewhere it came from,
somewhere it meant to go.

Magpies

So sure of yourselves
in all respects:
as meretricious
as a glossy mag. black and white page,
loud as a demagogue,
the most fanatic of parents,
with just that touch of blue sky
squeezed between single-minded
opposites in black and white.

I don't know where you fit
other than this very place
of shove-or-be-shoved
off the edge of urban daily life.
Your gifts, honed by those centuries
on wintry moors with shitten sheep
make you the number one survivor
in our obscene
Anthropocene patch
of concrete,
plastic-shrouded throwaways
and witches' chemical brews.

Gulls on a Football Pitch

The tide of day has brought gulls to a static sea.
Wheels of passing cars provide a constant surf.
Perhaps the gulls sense subtle motion in the earth.

Landlubber that I am
why do I feel at sea
walking the sterile pavements of this land
wishing I had a gull's adaptability
its calculated symmetry
its mastery of motion
on currents of land
or air or ocean?

ELEGAIC

Ode to a Cohabitant

Consider the architecture of trees
their structure, strength, design,
ability to house whole populations --
how they grace the graceless houses
of men in their concrete plantations
with the greens of their gentle roofs,
their columns observing proportion,
their good manners.

How, without fuss,
they mend themselves
using rain, sun,
the self-same earth
which bears us all
and, stripped,
reveal the secret
of their strength.

Once their cities covered where
ours now stand or where now
there is only sand.
Once they bound mountainsides,
beckoned the clouds.

With or without our consent
they will return,
allow us to sit beneath,
give those who remain
a second chance
to learn the art of standing.

Relic of War - 1

Spindle berries:
not glossed like holly's blood,
but pink as maiden's lips,
borne on these Spindle stems
that push against mossed brick
across the armoured concrete
of a bomb-proof roof,
casing stale dark
behind six menacing slits.

Another Christmas
ventures up the valley
against the river's flow.
another one not sure
what it will bring
though that particular war
was long ago.

These gentle berries
more kind than holly's,
not armed like hips,
held to the light
of a December sun
by this grim house of death,
plead to be seen,
be touched by stooping lips.

Relic of War – 2 – Resurrection

'Something there is that does not love a wall
That sends the frozen groundswell under it.'- Robert Frost

Wind, which harbours histories, speaks to these hill-top pines
of what this forest hides within its play of light and shade,
the thing it made its own down through these many years:
a Wall—stronger than Jericho,
high, wide as a house where no man ever lived,
long as a street without a destination,
built to keep nothing in, keep nothing out:
one might have said, "The paradox of a wall."

All that concrete, all that steel, the hauling, lifting,
laying down, the dedicated purpose, costing
such time, toil, and pain and all to prove if possibly
it might be razed by bombers, crossing a sea
to bomb its prototype, another tyrant's wall
in France, in Normandy.

At risk of death, dive bombers blasted holes,
but still, the wall stands,
adopted by young trees, their very own,
silently, solidly there, but subtly changed
and changing, into limestone cliff.

First water came, then ice, to break its veins,
abrade its skin, prepare a bed for seeds,
small plants, not native to this acid place:
fleabanes, hawkweeds, perfoliate penny cress,
berries of rowan, elder, roots of trees
snaking to split the man-made rock,
swayed by the wind, levering lumps apart.

Ants bore the grit away;
worms turned dead leaves to soil;
rust sapped the strength of steel;
the underminers – rabbits, weasels, mice,
the lodgers – redstarts, solitary wasps
and wrens, used shrapnel planter holes
and, night and day, a subtle alchemy
distilled the gold of life from man-made rock,
while clever fungal threads succoured new life
at depths that never saw the light.
The groundswell worked its invisible way.

Such histories, the pines convey
to those who stand below those lofty limbs,
which constantly invite the south-west wind
to play their harp, chanting a dark-toned lay.

Due Process

BANG !

Like paper scraps,
pigeons explode
at the November sky.
become pigeons again
wheeling in frantic arcs.

Shoppers panic
then grin,
embarrassed,
recalling date and time.

On the hill,
in stillness, choreographed,
spruce recruits,
smooth-faced,
sustain a silence
that is the other face
of violence.

Behind bright buttons
hearts throb.
Thoughts roam
behind eyes.

Then BANG ! again

But things are not the same:
the sun has moved a fraction.
Like a limb, severed,
a second hand jerks.
An autumn robin
squeezes in a bar
before the bugle sounds.

Rage and regimented silence
seem all that we can do.

Lacrimae Rerum (the tears of things)

Hip Hip Hooray, Hip Hip Hooray
the suburb's a hundred years old today.
Edith and Enid and George would know
if Edith and Enid and George could go
to the celebrations.

The plane trees are pruned
the railings painted
an ambulance ready
(though nobody fainted).
One hundred years you know!

Now boards and trestles are packed away.
Pigeons have cleared the crumbs,
cars will return to their parking,
small dogs to bouts of barking
at workmen building loft extensions.
Behind new double-glazing
widows fret about pensions.

Rain dribbles down the peeling bark
lamps emphasize the dark.
In unlit rooms, screens flicker.
Somewhere a robin ventures a song
while young women click and clatter
along in the gathering dusk
to empty two-room flats
and their up and down
waiting, purring, cats.

Oh Lacrimae
Lacrimae
dripping from twigs
of the hard-pruned plane
for a century long
of genteel pain.

Last Journey of Thomas Bewick's Swan

Within the oil lamp's glow,
bespectacled,
the engraver works his mystery:
hand touches wood;
wood conceives swan.

His swan, wild swan,
now floats upon a lake
proudly surveys her anchorage.
Her hand-chased plumage swells
beneath the shifting flame.

Drawing, he resurrects the dead:
once more he hears swans
calling through mist at dawn
like children out to play.

He cannot say
from what far coasts
these measured wings
have borne his swan,
over what icy seas
to this remembered land.

Thankful, but sad, he sighs,
sees January dawn
through frosted window-pane,
with wearied hand
lays down his instrument.

Perhaps, this very day
will bring his swans again,
calling like children.

Footnote: *Thomas Bewick (1753 – 1828) is widely acknowledged as the father of modern engraving. He was a gifted artist and passionately interested in country life and natural history. His engravings illustrate his texts and provide pictures of astonishing accuracy and tonal quality. In 1804, Volume 11 of his A History of British Birds was published, which focused on birds living on or near water. It is his picture in this volume of the smallest species of wild swan which brought him the honour of the swan being named after him. Bewick's Swan migrates from Siberian Russia to Western Europe and some eventually make it to Great Britain. Thomas Bewick observed and drew it in the area near Newcastle where he lived all his life. People in the area would bring him the bodies of birds they had found or shot. He was meticulous in his measurement of dead birds and his observation of those alive.*

The Quiet Side

Beyond the hill
soughs a daylong surf
of countless tyres
beating an endless road.

Tall masts,
that have no tides
to sway them here,
usurp the ridge.
Out of an emptiness
they trawl a ceaseless
babel to themselves.

But here and now
a south wind
strokes the misty down,
and sky as pale as clay
harbours a voice
too innocent
for clever snares.

Against all odds,
one tiny lark proclaims
faith has been kept
with the returning Spring.

Master Class

Teach me, black bird
with yellow orange bill
what tree, what twig to choose
what moment of the day
how best to train the singing parts
to throw my song
across a field, a wood
a garden or a park
to find a human ear
a passage to the heart
with intonations,
pauses, subtle turns
familiar phrasing
yet never quite the same
and all without a single word.

When The Wild Geese Fly that Way

Wild geese on the hillside stubble
are noisy as boys in a yard.
But see them now,
thrusting high over the town
in perfect arrow formation
calling a different tune.
Wondering, the pale-faced boys gaze up,
silenced, longing with them to fly.

Frugality of a Bird

Take for example
the dunnock
so hesitant so shy
picking in winter
beneath dry stems
of lavender
from here
from there
a fallen seed
a desiccated fly
a crumb from someone's feast
to feed its hollow bones
its ceaseless search
its sweet fragmented song
thanking the February sun.

ARMORICA (Cornwall across the Sea)

Misty summer Sunday morning

Still as an owl's egg
here is a tangible waiting
a time when dreams
like ancient carp
have settled in their pools.

Maize so still, so tall,
will grow no taller,
points pale fingers at nothing,
still as green marble
as a babe not to be wakened
or stirred by the slightest breath
of a pausing breeze.

Even the crow in his oak
who does not sleep
is content to stay
does not fly to the top of the fir
to announce new day
in his time-honoured way.

This is a dawn soundless as space
at peace with itself
without ambition.

Glow Worms

Rain, after drought,
has washed the August sky.
Stars, in their flocks uncountable
browse the huge bowl of heaven
beyond the tumbling satellites
and planes striving to destinations.

Their healing reaches to the harvest field
soothing the raked stubble,
the little creatures of this little earth.

On the moist margins of the road
snails creep skywards;
the white Campion shows pale,
and there and there
keeping a tryst,
you find another miracle:
a colony of pulsing gems
wooing their sister stars
with constellations of more gentle fire.

Canticle of the Tidal Mud

Vide St. Francis' Canticle of the Sun

Birds are the words,
the voices of this intertidal plain,
waiting, watching, settling,
as they do, by one or two
and then by thousands,
sharing bird information
on the tidal situation.

Oh, the excitement,
the unleashed energy of it all
at bidding of sun and moon:
oyster catchers piping,
terns calling one to another,
herring gull's chuckle and laugh,
plaint of plover,
silence of great black gull.

Then, swift and sweeping
from the North
descend the aerial hosts,
deceiving human sight
in wheeling, flickering flight -
dunlin and knot,
the restless sanderling:
wings and feet in their thousands,
to reap the harvest of life
begotten in this in vitro mud.

But day is done,
'My Brethren, Enough!'
(Saint Francis' salutation)
'Water has won back land,

there's small space left to stand.
Your myriad wings
must take to air.'

Wavelets now lap the stone
of this small harbour wall,
watched by the local gull
who, from her birth,
has known the triple pull
of sun and moon and earth.

And as the starling hosts
at dying of day
scroll messages on skies,
some poet has traced in mud
along the slate-capped wall
these lines:

'When tide is once more out,
and miles of mud appear,
Please let me shout
"Behold the womb of life!"'

Refugees

Here, strip of salt sand
between high water
and High Road,
now squat on by these
whose one imperative
is 'Stay alive.
Keep heads, eyes, down.
Do not be seen
by the established powers.'

'Untidy lot!'
The powers would say,
'not here tomorrow
if we had our way.
With concrete, engines
brass,
you can move mountains
in a day and shovel all
this sordidness away.'

Meanwhile the world will spin
and elements persist
whom even the powers cannot resist
so well as these self-taught,
visa-less, no man's landers:

marram, cotton grass, mouse ear,
the savage horizontal rose,
sow-thistle, ragworts
and their attendant snails,
gracing the skeleton arms
of blanched sea-lavender,
their dried life-juices
gluing empty shells.

Touching the primordial

This vast expanse of mud surrendered by the sea
has helped me recognise
those powers that shape our being
and our will, that work, some say
through moon and sun
and liquid iron of earth's core.

How cunningly they work the tides
of water, blood and sap of tree,
of air, of stratosphere and so-called 'Space'.

Some say that we emerged from fecund slime
much like this ribbed and puddled anonymity,
holding the sky in mirrors,
nourished by sea two times a day.
Is anything out there concerned with what they say?

No answer from the silence of the bay,
unless you call the rumour of a tide
too far away to see, an answer,
or wind-snatched cry of gull.

How many realms of meaning are there
in a seabird's cry?
How many words of all the languages
that ever man spoke or wrote
before the dictionaries
with all their derivations, definitions, connotations.

ELSEWHERE

Signs and Selfies

Bushmen, they say
could read the signs
that others could not read –
those others from the North,
Hottentot, Boer and alien Us.

Their signs:
the talking book of stars
dust devil's dance
honey bird's call
dreams of the Ancestors.

But we, the ear-lobed deaf,
makers of mindless din,
wasters and litterers,
blinders of stars,
read only ourselves
posing on backgrounds
like hunters on something killed.

Silver Birches outside Moscow

Caught by an early snow
along the forest edge
these silver birches
stand in frozen pirouettes –
unpartnered ballerinas
on a barren stage
against a backdrop of dark firs.

The flaking tatters of their bark
seamlessly spun,
catch dawn's brief dye.

Perhaps this fall
will melt today
and under restless stars
they will resume their dance
before real winter comes,
then sleep the sleep only trees know
throughout the dreadful tyranny of snow.

Hot day on the Embankment

Hot June day –
butterflies flitting
butterfly girls skipping
tripping along pavements
by the Thames
pausing, almost, here
perching almost, there
to sip at this or that delight.

Such quickened energy
fed with the nectar of novelty.
Such happy carelessness
whilst solemn tides flow in
flow out, as moon dictates.

Such frangible, tangible, transience.
Such powered constancy
juxtaposed -
the plane trees tremble and sigh.

Unsolved

Somewhere, high in these March woods
the Yaffle sees off winter
with a mocking laugh.

Once long ago, I found his body
before the ants could colonise
the splendour of his clothes -
Gold, scarlet, green:
green for the coming spring
scarlet and gold for summer.
(though life's blood is red
there was no sign of struggle.)

From the helmet of his head
poked the spiral of his tongue
as from a broken watch – too much
of hammering perhaps?

The woods are good at keeping schtoom.
Who knows?
There are those who say
someone had his revenge.

Footnote: *Picus viridis, the Green Woodpecker, known to some Englishmen as the Yaffle, has a very long tongue coiled within his skull. This helps to cushion the blows of hammering holes.*

Incident at Noon

'Where would we be without gravity?'
he said, in his old man's voice,
beneath the acacia tree,
looking towards the hills
he could not see.

In the red dust, I saw his spectacles,
placed them back in his restless hands.
He was not surprised –
in his world, things did what they pleased.

Bees hummed, bright finches busied
themselves amongst the acacia flowers:
creatures with wings!

All that humming and the heat -
I must have dozed.
His stick, vital third leg,
lay in the dust. He was not there.

I sat and pondered,
weighing each possibility,
'til only one remained –
his opening remark –
came back and back
like a bothering fly:
Where would we be without gravity?
Where would we be?

Above, thorns held no fluttering reply.
The pale sky was empty.

Urban Ecology

No-one tore them down.
Only snails
discreet as night
and rain
not so discreet
eroded the poems
posted that year
along the street.

But some
who were passing by
paused
made out a fading line
or two
passed on,
unwitting carriers
of the word
lodged like a virus
in the brain
or seed
in crack of stone.

And maybe
when new rain
urges the seed
to break its tomb
to utter flowers
from the stone
the snails will fail to wake
and words like wallflowers
wallflowers like words
will catch the eye
of a new season's
passer-by.

Ecumenical Moment

One of those January afternoons
when starlings,
as though they'll never cease,
wheeze, whistle, bleat, bubble
gurgle, ratchet hymns of praise
to a brief, beneficent sun.

No hymn sheets here,
though something of the church
in these high wintering limes
outside the graveyard wall –
no verse, no vestment.

Here they have settled
on leafless boughs,
a multi-lingual host,
resplendent, iridescent,
envy of angels in this
gift of winter sun.

What would the Dean have done
were such a choir inside -
two hundred fervent Zoroastrians
with uncoordinated bills?

Clock on church tower strikes four:
solemn reverberating tones
command a vacuum
which utter silence fills.

Not a note now,
not a single floating feather,
even the sun has gone,
resigned to proper January weather.

Rural Canvas

This curving Down
now roughly shaved,
its crushed and crumbled chalk
ground to a base,
receives the evening light
pink as a painter's wash
ready for his design.
Hedges trace shadows
down wavering edges.

Autumn comes and goes,
in corners and margins
leaves sketches of hips and haws
Old Man's Beard,
vignettes of rooks and daws.

Winter sits heavy and long
at the easel,
wrestling with clichés
for Christmas cards
while the earth rests.
Come Spring,
the painter's wash demands
a statement of some kind –
Say, colour after rain,
of new-turned soil,
a burgeoning crop?

But what is this in June?
What will the critics say?
Perhaps it'll go away -
Enough to make Van Gogh swoon,
paint wheels of fire,
self-consume.

As you come over the hill
this YELLOW grabs your eye:
yellow of Oilseed Rape –
Good name for something
that came at night
and seized the subtle beauty
of this southern Down.

Give me the paler shades of barley,
wheat or oats,
moved by the clouds that cross an English sky
and keep this upstart yellow
for eyes in galleries
of a smaller size.

THE TESTING SHORES

A Slanting Land

Slate burdened
quartz riven
slanting land,
arrowed from seas
where winds begin
beyond the setting sun.

Here, angled iron
splits rock,
the broken bones of thorn
set east.
Men struggle,
bent to slopes
before a driven rain.

No vertical,
no angle right,
no given plane:
all's wrought
out of an ancient awkwardness
spelled to this dissident beauty.

Wool on the Wire

Up here
sheep feed
on wire-wool grass,
rock's tears,
air.
They never cease chewing.

The bones of their jaws
strengthen walls
where gates
at lower levels sag.

From the day
their dried-out mothers
move away,
to their night of dying
they never cease chewing.

Stoic, anonymous philosophers,
ingesting all the inventory
of shifting light:
lost wanderers,
curlew, cloud,
reducing all to notions
vague as mist --
conclusions no more certain
than the destinations
of their timeless trails
weaving the moor.

Exhibition in Port

Spent, vaguely satisfied,
tide withdraws.
Framed between cliffs,
breakwater, sky,
a collage, her work,
lies on washed sand
to dry.

Connoisseur gulls
adopt old vantage points,
note how the tilted boats
have new relationships,
how weed's green olive
is dabbed today,
how water has laid
its new small dead
amongst a shining jewellery
of slate, glass, brick,
rust welded with salt.

Obliquely, autumn sun
sends out an invitation.
Careless as pirates
people invade the scene –
dog grabs dead dogfish;
children hunt colours and shapes;
a woman turns slivers of wood
distressed by salt and sea:
Booty for everyone.

But days grow short,
light dims, tide turns.
World turns,
craving novelty.

Yelping, the knowing gulls
peel, each from his station,
in search of a new sensation.

Raven's Gratitude

Bird of few words
the raven,
but sincere.
Croaks thanks
for the thorn tree's
shelter from the blast.
Croaks for the currents
that lift him above the world.
Croaks at dawn on the shore
that bears the neap tide's gifts.
Croaks for the verticality of rock
shielding his young,
Croaks for his faithful mate
and five perfect eggs.
Croaks for the lamb
dropped in a bitter Spring
and the bleached bones
of the dam who bore it.

Fulmar

Above this haunting, echoing cove
where fern and lichen cling to weeping rock
too steep to house the gulls
that wail and mock,
the jewel eyed fulmar
rides his realm of air
as though all perils there
were made for his delight.

Meantime, his mate
with white and gleaming breast
sits at her cliff-hole nest
defying shadows dark as night,
the sure and only haven
to guide his homing flight.

Estuary

Ebb tide slows to no tide --
motionless, on her perch,
bows of a sunken barge,
Morvran, black crow of the sea,
hangs out her wings
to dry –
gaunt coat of arms.

Off stage,
behind the little port
the young moon waits
to summon back the sea.

Morvran lives in three worlds:
on water, under water,
in the sky.
Now I am part of her sky-world,
hunch-shouldered on the shore,
looking at her –
she watches me.

She knows her space,
how in a while the dusk will come
to render everything less definite than I.

How voices of those who drowned
will call from the open sea --
the ghosts of those who perished
down the years
when tide turned silently,

came surging back across the bar,
rolling their little boats to death
in choking foam –
so near, so infinitely far
from waiting home.

Michael Tanner – Biography

Michael Tanner was born in 1933, the second of four children. He was evacuated at the age of seven but returned to Bristol before the end of the blitz. A new baby put all his mother's resilience to the test. His father, ex trooper, was invalided back to Blighty in WW1. and became an ARP Warden in the evenings.

Michael has two sons and a daughter from his first marriage and another son and stepson from his remarriage after the tragic death of his first wife. His daughter gave him a granddaughter. He ran nine London marathons and remains a keen amateur naturalist.

His Bristol B.A. was followed by National Service, mostly as a subaltern serving with the K.A.R. in Kenya. After that he trained as a teacher and taught, mainly English, for 38 years, at secondary schools, meanwhile obtaining a B.A. Hons English at Birkbeck. Most of his spare time he writes, and squeezes in study of foreign languages, and trying to play the clarinet.

He feels much gratitude to many, especially his parents and a diminutive, asthmatic Scotsman, who taught him English at Grammar School.

Palewell Press

Palewell Press is an independent publisher handling poetry, fiction and non-fiction with a focus on books that foster Justice, Equality and Sustainability. The Editor can be reached on enquiries@palewellpress.co.uk

Lightning Source UK Ltd.
Milton Keynes UK
UKHW020846290820
369024UK00005B/183

9 781911 587361